Mastering Project Management Tools

*Streamlining Tasks, Deadlines,
and Team Collaboration*

Preface

Understanding The Problem

In today's fast-paced business environment, managing projects efficiently is more important than ever. However, many teams struggle with disorganized tasks, poor communication, and missed deadlines. This eBook, "Mastering Project Management Tools: Streamlining Tasks, Deadlines, and Team Collaboration," aims to provide a comprehensive guide to overcoming these challenges using modern project management tools.

IMPORTANCE OF EFFECTIVE PROJECT MANAGEMENT

Effective project management is crucial for the success of any organization. It ensures that tasks are completed on time, resources are used efficiently, and team members are working collaboratively towards common goals. By leveraging project management tools, you can transform the way you manage projects and achieve greater success.

I hope this guide serves as a valuable resource in helping you understand, set up, and maximize the benefits of project management tools. Whether you are new to project management or looking to enhance your existing practices, this book offers insights and practical advice to help you succeed.

Thank you for choosing this book. Let's embark on this journey to master project management tools together.

Warm regards,

Asif Tourab

AUTHOR'S INTRODUCTION

Hello, dear reader!

My name is Asif Tourab, and I am excited to guide you through the world of project management tools. With a background in cybersecurity, I have seen firsthand how effective project management can transform an organization's operations. My professional experience has shown me the importance of using the right tools to manage tasks, deadlines, and team collaboration.

The inspiration for this book came from my own challenges with project management and the frequent inquiries I received from colleagues and clients about how to improve their project management practices. Project management tools have revolutionized the way we handle projects, offering solutions to many of the common problems associated with traditional methods.

This book is designed to be a comprehensive guide, providing you with everything you need to know about project management tools. From understanding the basics to exploring advanced features, I aim to equip you with the knowledge and tools to make informed decisions and optimize your project management practices.

Thank you for embarking on this journey with me. I hope you find this book informative and empowering.

Sincerely,

Asif Tourab

TABLE OF CONTENTS

1. Introduction
2. Chapter 1: The Challenges of Project Management
3. Chapter 2: What Are Project Management Tools?
4. Chapter 3: Benefits of Using Project Management Tools
5. Chapter 4: Choosing the Right Project Management Tool
6. Chapter 5: Setting Up Your Project Management Tool
7. Chapter 6: Effective Task Management
8. Chapter 7: Enhancing Team Collaboration
9. Chapter 8: Advanced Features and Customization
10. Chapter 9: Maintaining Your Project Management Tool
11. Conclusion
12. Appendix

INTRODUCTION

Understanding The Importance Of Project Management Tools

In the fast-paced world of modern business, effective project management is essential to ensure that tasks are completed on time, within budget, and to the desired quality standards. However, many organizations struggle with disorganized project tasks, poor team collaboration, and missed deadlines. This eBook, "Mastering Project Management Tools: Streamlining Tasks, Deadlines, and Team Collaboration," aims to provide a comprehensive guide to overcoming these challenges using the latest project management tools.

The Evolution Of Project Management

Project management has evolved significantly over the years, from manual methods using pen and paper to sophisticated digital tools that offer a plethora of features. These tools are designed to help teams collaborate more effectively, manage tasks efficiently, and meet deadlines consistently. Understanding how to leverage these tools can transform the way you manage projects and lead to greater success.

CHAPTER 1: THE CHALLENGES OF PROJECT MANAGEMENT

Disorganized Project Tasks

One of the biggest challenges in project management is keeping tasks organized. Without a clear system in place, tasks can easily become scattered, leading to confusion and inefficiency. This disorganization can result in important tasks being overlooked or delayed.

Poor Team Collaboration

Effective collaboration is crucial for successful project management. However, many teams struggle with poor communication and lack of coordination. This can lead to misunderstandings, duplicated efforts, and a decrease in overall productivity.

Missed Deadlines And Delayed Projects

When tasks are not managed properly and team collaboration is lacking, it is common for deadlines to be missed and projects to be delayed. This not only affects the project at hand but can also damage the reputation of the organization and lead to financial losses.

CHAPTER 2: WHAT ARE PROJECT MANAGEMENT TOOLS?

Definition And Overview

Project management tools are software applications designed to assist in planning, organizing, and managing resources to achieve project goals. These tools provide a central platform for task management, team collaboration, and tracking progress, ensuring that projects are completed efficiently and effectively.

Key Features Of Project Management Tools

CHAPTER 3: BENEFITS OF USING PROJECT MANAGEMENT TOOLS

Enhanced Organization

Project management tools help to centralize all project-related information, making it easier to keep track of tasks, deadlines, and resources. This leads to better organization and reduces the risk of important details being overlooked.

Improved Collaboration

With integrated communication tools, file sharing capabilities, and real-time updates, project management tools enhance team collaboration. This ensures that all team members are on the same page and can work together effectively.

Timely Project Completion

By providing tools for task management, time tracking, and resource allocation, project management tools help ensure that projects are completed on time and within budget. This leads to higher client satisfaction and better project outcomes.

CHAPTER 4: CHOOSING THE RIGHT PROJECT MANAGEMENT TOOL

Assessing Your Needs

Before selecting a project management tool, it is important to assess your specific needs. Consider factors such as the size of your team, the complexity of your projects, and the features you require.

Comparing Popular Tools

There are many project management tools available, each with its own strengths and weaknesses. Popular options include Trello, Asana, Monday.com, and Jira. Compare these tools based on features, ease of use, and cost to find the best fit for your needs.

Cost Considerations

Project management tools come with various pricing models, from free versions with limited features to premium subscriptions. Consider your budget and the value that the tool will bring to your organization when making a decision.

CHAPTER 5: SETTING UP YOUR PROJECT MANAGEMENT TOOL

Creating An Account

The first step in setting up a project management tool is creating an account. This typically involves providing basic information and choosing a subscription plan.

Setting Up Projects And Tasks

Once your account is set up, start by creating your first project. Add tasks, set deadlines, and assign them to team members. Organize tasks into categories or lists to keep everything structured.

Integrating With Other Tools

Many project management tools offer integrations with other software applications, such as email, calendars, and file storage services. Set up these integrations to streamline your workflow and enhance productivity.

CHAPTER 6: EFFECTIVE TASK MANAGEMENT

Assigning And Prioritizing Tasks

Assign tasks to the appropriate team members and set priorities to ensure that the most important tasks are completed first. Use labels, tags, or color-coding to indicate priority levels.

Tracking Progress And Deadlines

Regularly monitor the progress of tasks and ensure that deadlines are being met. Use features such as Gantt charts or Kanban boards to visualize progress and identify any potential delays.

Automating Routine Tasks

Many project management tools offer automation features that can help streamline repetitive tasks. Use these features to automate routine processes, such as sending reminders or updating task statuses.

CHAPTER 7: ENHANCING TEAM COLLABORATION

Communication Tools

Effective communication is key to successful project management. Use built-in communication tools, such as chat, comments, and @mentions, to keep team members informed and engaged.

File Sharing And Document Collaboration

Easily share files and collaborate on documents directly within your project management tool. This ensures that all team members have access to the latest versions and can work together in real-time.

Real-Time Updates And Notifications

Keep everyone up-to-date with real-time updates and notifications. Set up alerts for task assignments, deadline changes, and important milestones to ensure that nothing is missed.

CHAPTER 8: ADVANCED FEATURES AND CUSTOMIZATION

Gantt Charts And Timelines

Gantt charts and timelines provide a visual representation of your project schedule, making it easier to track progress and identify potential bottlenecks. Customize these views to suit your project's needs.

Custom Workflows And Automation

Create custom workflows to match your project's specific processes. Use automation features to streamline tasks, such as moving tasks between stages or sending automated updates.

Reporting And Analytics

Generate detailed reports and analyze project performance using built-in reporting tools. Use these insights to make data-driven decisions and improve future project planning.

CHAPTER 9: MAINTAINING YOUR PROJECT MANAGEMENT TOOL

Regular Updates And Maintenance

Keep your project management tool updated with the latest features and security patches. Regular maintenance ensures that the tool runs smoothly and efficiently.

Managing User Permissions And Access

Control who has access to your projects and what permissions they have. Set up user roles and access levels to protect sensitive information and ensure that team members have the appropriate level of access.

Troubleshooting Common Issues

Familiarize yourself with common issues and their solutions. This will help you quickly resolve problems and maintain smooth operation of your project management tool.

CONCLUSION

Recap Of Key Points

Project management tools offer a centralized platform for managing tasks, deadlines, and team collaboration. By leveraging these tools, you can enhance organization, improve collaboration, and ensure timely project completion.

Encouragement To Implement Project Management Tools

Take the first step towards better project management by choosing and implementing a project management tool that fits your needs. Experience the benefits of streamlined tasks, improved collaboration, and successful project outcomes.

APPENDIX

Frequently Asked Questions

Glossary Of Terms

www.ingramcontent.com/pod-product-compliance
Lightning Source LLC
Chambersburg PA
CBHW071222240526
45470CB00018B/2291